Gold Conjuring Poetry

Gold is a living god and rules in scorn,
All earthly things but virtue

~ *Percy Bysshe Shelley*

Also by Angel Edwards

Tales in the Dreams Garden (Silver Bow)
Lust Unfiltered by Love (Silver Bow)
Spirits Dressed Up as Poems (Silver Bow)

Gold Conjuring Poetry

Angel Edwards

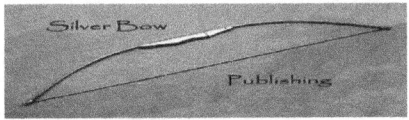

Silver Bow Publishing
720 Sixth St., Unit #5
New Westminster, BC V3L3C5
CANADA

Title: Gold Conjuring Poetry
Author: Angel Edwards
Publisher: Silver Bow Publishing
Cover Design: Candice James
Editing & Layout: Candice James

All rights reserved including the right to reproduce or translate this book or any portions thereof, in any form without the permission of the publisher. Except for the use of short passages for review purposes, no part of this book may be reproduced, in part or in whole, or transmitted in any form or by any means, electronically or mechanically, including photocopying, recording, or any information or storage retrieval system without prior permission in writing from the publisher or a license from the Canadian Copyright Collective Agency (Access Copyright).

www.silverbowpublishing.com
info@silverbowpublishing.com
© silver bow publishing

Library and Archives Canada Cataloguing in Publication

Title: Gold conjuring poetry / Angel Edwards.
Names: Edwards, Angel, 1952- author.
Description: Poems.
Identifiers: Canadiana (print) 20200219294 | Canadiana (ebook) 20200219308 | ISBN 9781774030943
   (softcover) | ISBN 9781774030950 (HTML)
Classification: LCC PS8609.D834 G65 2020 | DDC C811/.6—dc23

Table of Contents

Gold Leaf Tobacco ... 7
24 Karat Joint ... 8
Gold in Their Leaves ... 9
Gold Guitar Notes ... 10
Golding ... 11
Prince Edward-Golden Haired Heir ... 12
Gold Picnic ... 13
1334 A.D. ... 14
A Village of Gold ... 15
A Winter's Money Spell ... 16
Achaean Rocks ... 17
Albeit ... 18
Cambodian Sunset Ruby ... 19
Celebrate ... 20
Extravagance ... 21
Flower Show ... 22
Fools' Gold ... 23
Gold Bullets ... 24
Gold Diggers ... 25
Gold Panning ... 26
Golden Calf ... 27
Golden Crown ...28
Gold, Golden Gold ... 29
Haniel Gold Light ... 30
Heart of Greed ... 31
Ill-gotten ... 32
Iniquity ... 33
King Louis the Glorious Sun King ... 34
Life Inside a Diamond Room ... 35
Lost Golden Soul ... 36
Lovebirds in Gold Feathers ... 37
Miser ... 38
Moon Village ... 39
Second Rate Imitation ... 40
Silver Tongue, Golden Voice ... 41
Sky Castle ... 42
Sun ... 43

10 Karat Gold Covers ... 44
The Gold Ballroom ... 45
The Golden Age ... 46
The Golden Owl Heirloom ... 47
The Heist ... 48
To Awaken the Sleeping Dragon ... 49
Topaz Gem ... 50
Useless Treasure ... 51
Wigs and Gold Soles ... 52
Golden Wolf Eyes ... 53
Perfect Replicas ... 54
One Gold Tear ... 55
Think About Money with Affection ... 56
Spell to Attract Gold ... 57
Buttercups and Goldenseal ... 58
The Fool and the Magician ... 59
Crown Chakra ... 60
Heart of Gold ... 61
Greed ... 62
Inside a Gold Vault ... 63
Mountain of Gold ... 64
The Minotaur ... 65

Gold Leaf Tobacco

Fragrant tobacco smoke

pipe tobacco, pure tobacco
rolled from the leaves

gold leaf premium
far away plantation
centuries-old process
bites the throat
grasps the breath
seductive soothing
somehow pleasurable

meditative with each inhale
relaxing with each exhale

golden red embers
half burned logs

a glow cast
to ignite the shadows

dark wooden walls
side lit

antique gold
candle powered lamps

24 Karat Joint

rose gold kush
Acapulco gold
Columbian gold
black gold

purple gold sativa
gold veined blue island hybrid
wrapped snuggly inside
24 karat gold leaf
rolling paper

sleeping
awaiting
your lips and fire

Gold in Their Leaves

ode to all you
magnificent eucalyptus trees

particles of gold exist
within your healing leaves

thirsting for water your roots extend
miles below the surface

respect and love to healing trees
their essences sustain us

Gold Guitar Notes

gold guitar notes
plucked on upper neck
tiny
tinny
treble sound

thumping bass
adding suspense
half notes descending

song within
wordless

played on lower frets
gold guitar notes

Golding

Gilded golding into golden
an immeasurable token
stumbling on a diamond wall,
in a ruby waterfall.

Gleaming Sapphire and starshine,
jagged amethyst terrain
cutting, slicing my footsteps,
bleeding without any pain.

Golden dusted, gold embossed,
lapis crusted, moonstone frost.
Onyx night now fully sated
Emerges gilded and gold plated.

Caught on fire inside dawn's holding
they've become the final golding.

Prince Edward-Golden Haired Heir

Prince Edward,
baby king,
never allowed to be a child.

Golden curls, golden crown,
golden destiny
short lived.

Difficult for a child to be 'good' all the time.

If he strayed ever,
if he broke any rule
his whipping boy would receive punishment.

Tormented the child
but he had to comply,
obey as he was the heir.

Prince Edward the child played with toys of solid gold.
He wore garments sewn with gold and silver thread:
Uncomfortable stiff clothes.
Uncomfortable stiff manners.
Never really allowed to run free.
Extremely restrained
almost as if he were a little puppet
instead of a boy.

Long awaited birth of the male heir to the tyrant king.
Prince Edward no tyrant; innocent.

Short sweet reign.

Gold Picnic

gold picnic with champagne
gold rimmed crystal glasses
gold honeycomb
    saffron soft bread
    devilled eggs
    yellow cake lemon icing

honeyed peeled
gold apples
cold corn bread
two bananas
yellow sun hat

    sandy tender kisses
    gold and blue sundress
    yellow beach blanket
    sporting gold sun design

golden summer sun a-shine
golden July

1334 A.D.

as Queen Joanna of Navarre
rode through Cheapside

six lucky musicians from Suffolk
paraded alongside

performed in procession
displayed skill and pride

they received 13 shillings
plus four-pence

King Henry IV
Spared no expense

A Village of Gold

A village of gold
dazzles in the sun still
blinds at daybreak
steals away sleep

villagers nibble gold wine
tremble inside their cold gold abodes

golden tongued everyone
uttered by all
to render these voices void
devoid of value

gold thread spun
making gold attire
heavy gold thread
embroidered gold robes

torturous teetering gold shoes

a village of gold
dazzles in the sun still
blinds by daybreak
steals away peace

A Winter's Money Spell

come break of dawn mid-winter
cast a money drawing spell
frankincense cinnamon
four rings of a silver bell

gold thread silver thread
to a green velvet scarf sewn
three antique coins
wearing royal head
light one gold candle alone
think lovingly of wealth
drink to Gold's health

Achaean Rocks

Achaean rocks
more than 2.5 billion years old
frequently contain,
possess, retain gold.

Inside huge stars
gold is created
as stars explode,
become supernovas.
They give birth to gold.

Gold traveled on asteroids,
hitched a ride to earth
upon quartz host rocks,

The time measure
beyond human.

Irrelevant clocks.

Albeit

Gilded gold, golden.
Immeasurable token.

A blinding reflection.
Gold in every direction.

Stumbling upon
a diamond well
sheltered inside
a pillar of gold
ruby rivers
of water fell.

Storm reached beyond
safe albeit cold.

A blinding reflection.
Gold in every direction.

Cambodian Sunset Ruby

Cambodian sunset,
ruby cloudiness to disguise the value.

The art lurks in the tender slicing.

Cut the rock to the core.
Expose the jewel in hiding.

Celebrate

Celebrate

a joint rolled
24 karat gold
yellow gold paper

moby dick
golden cobra
scoutmaster

Celebrate

Extravagance

The vintage Rolls Royce
was not her ride of choice

red velvet interior
lush ebony and mahogany

made her feel inferior
an imposter

a peasant without a voice
drowning in luxury

newly added GPS
handsome chauffeur haughty cold

her extravagant velvet royal blue dress
tumbling gold curls adorned

diamond sprinkles crystal stars
emerald aquamarine bracelet
black pearl agate ring on middle finger
Cinderella shoes of uncomfortable glass
red wine belle of the ball

penultimate dance
fifteen-hour feast
extravagance

Flower Show

They were goldenrods

yellow roses
sunflowers striking poses,

We were gold lilies

gilt faced tulips
blonde ladies sipping juleps.

Fools' Gold

jaded love this fools' gold
iron pyrite of the heart
jaded love treacherous
mis-stepping fallen apart

jaded love shaded fades
pinching the tender nerve
faithless romance
jaded hate parades
just what they deserve

close together hand in hand
lapis lazuli friend of gold
stone cold lovers dance
jaded embrace
entwine unfold

jaded love this fools' gold

Gold Bullets

gold bullets reside inside a gun
covered steel enclosed in
24 karat gold

lays smooth upon the palm
yet effortful to hold

gold bullets were fired inside
an armored car of 18 karat gold
gold concealed in steel

plans fell to the wayside
failed big time
gone wrong big deal

Gold Diggers

heartbreak suspended
within a diamond vial
ravaged, rouged face
speaks no denial

iron pyrite pirate
feet of clay fools' gold
counterfeit coins
bought, lost, re sold

flash contrived lover
brash gold-digging fool
cavalier courtships
calculating cold cruel

empty handed in the end
forlorn and still greed-obsessed
jewels smashed into small stones
lush grand palace repossessed

Gold Panning

eight backbreaking hours
stooping over the chilly stream

glimpse of gold
glittering
materializing
the gold panniers dream

Golden Calf

golden calf
days of olden

gold calf
God had the last laugh

its head human size
body of gilded veal
the dead ruby eyes
stamped with a golden seal

is extraordinary
is desultory

Golden Crown

Take this heavy crown from my head;
the gold feels like it is made of lead.
I am besieged bedeviled with this migraine.

I do not lay claim to this throne.
I do not wish to wear the crown.
My brain is wracked in horrific pain.

Chains of kingship pummel me down.
I am compelled to wear this crown.

I cannot endure the weight.
I would abdicate now
but it is too late.

Ancient golden metal
adored as divine splendor.

Debilitating golden amour
possesses the weary wearer.

Gold, Golden Gold

gold, golden gold
impermeable indestructible
magnificent malleable
moldable shapeable
jaw dropping adorable

worshipped desired
to die for
to kill for

shiny mesmerizing
blinding spell binding

valuable ancient
money measure
equitable equity
assured riches
insured wealth
timeless treasure

gold
gold
gold

golden gold

Haniel Gold Light

conception of creation
joyous manifestation

turquoise rays
splashed in green
gold light prances
       in between

full moon smiles at Venus
prays Haniel will see us

Heart of Greed

Guilty of the love of lucre
an avaricious heart of greed
caged within an endless urge
of unfulfilled grasping need.

Ill-gotten

They walked in glee
through the pile of dollar bills.

American hundred-dollar bills
thousands of them
by any count.

The couple were pleased.
Their ill-gotten fortune
caused them no remorse,
no guilt.

Unmarked bills,
no bloodshed.
Mr. and Mrs.
proud of their booty.

Iniquity
haiku

molten liquid gold
valued through iniquity
pure form of money

King Louis the Glorious Sun King

King Louis the glorious sun king
original sunny day speech
lived in the palace of gold
while basic livelihood
became out of reach
out of touch
living in his own
precious orbit
his subjects starving
oblivious to it
theatrical throned-playwright
star producer brilliance
upstaging anything of importance
his every move
observed applauded
absurd live entertainment
the netflix of centuries past.

King Louis the bright Sun King.
Rock star zillionaire.
Ownership entitlement.
Surpassing measure.
Versailles veritable treasure.

Life Inside a Diamond Room

three walls of rough diamonds
a gold velvet fainting chair
sky blue painted ceiling
room that really isn't there

table made of crystal quartz
three plates gold silver mix
silver candy dish offers
diamonds and amethysts

ruby cherries
liquid gold unable to drink
sapphire blueberries
nightmare room I cannot think

Lost Golden Soul

He was born with a golden soul
lost somehow along the rocky road of life.

He wandered empty, forlorn
throughout the world
searching for his lost soul.

He could not sleep.
He was restless
always hunting.
He could not eat.
He had no appetite.

Empty of desire for women and men.
No desire for anything
except his missing soul.

One night, dreaming wide awake,
he had a vision.
His soul was contained in a little house
occupied by a beautiful woman.

In over bloom
at the top of a hill,
his golden soul
locked inside an ebony trunk.

No key could open it.

Lovebirds in Gold Feathers
(haiku)

Lovebirds in gold suits
trimmed in green kissed by feathers
blue teardrops cascade

Miser

A dismal, poignant, pungent air.
Heavy bags of empty bottles and cans.
Long stringy unwashed greying hair.
Dirt embossed claw like hands.
Scabby face, runny nose,
vacant blinking stare,
body clad in tattered filthy clothes.

The look of someone
who has stayed out in the rain,
impervious to the weather.
Seemingly numb to pain.

The truth is, he is a miser.
He is eternally poor in his head.

Unused bills worth tens of thousands
hiding beneath his decrepit bed.

Moon Village

A space project named "Moon Village",
mission of robotic astronaut deployment.
Will the world come together,
our earthly differences to circumvent?

Communication satellites
upon the lunar south pole,
four story inflatable modules,
are pace high-rises the goal?

Go beyond the stars:
unprecedented academic sprint,
3 D protective shields,
robots commissioned to print.

Around the skyscrapers,
pressurized walkways
tied to air locks
change our perception of nights and days.

Shackleton crater ridge.
Go further into space.
Witness the moon's invisible face,
the moon's secret face.

Permanent lunar settlement:
expandable, adaptable.

Next full moon is a blue moon here.

Can humanity cast our differences aside?
All are welcome who are able to pay.
The Moon Road Ride
opens in May.

Second Rate Imitation

turn coal into diamonds
transform lead into gold
a philosopher's stone
story commonly told

in year 2020
it can be achieved
second rate imitation
man-made yet achieved.

Silver Tongue, Golden Voice

silver tongue
        golden voice
quicksilver wit
        sapphire tears
ruby blood droplets

        gift of the gab
celestial song
        diamond sharp mind
jaded jade heart

Sky Castle

standing unscathed
        castle made of gold
windows of diamonds
        unmoving in the wind
kissed by the moon

none sit upon the throne
        unruled unloved
frigid realm
        proudly solitary

sea birds
        blinded at the sight
do not perch there
        or visit
the wild ocean below
        cannot harm nor modify
through ages, eons, centuries
        sky-castle sentinel stays

Sun
(haiku)

Winter sunshine reigns
yellow golden dominance
cloudless obeyance

10 Karat Gold Covers

Their shapely essence
preserved beneath metal
bouquet of flowers
lily of the valley
roses, one daffodil
ten karat gold covers

they remain for a longer spell

encapsulated floral lives
strange springtime ritual

The Gold Ballroom

Inside a well-kept heritage manor
hides a luxurious ball room.

Walls and floors
are 24 karat gold.

The ceilings
are painted pale yellow.

Tiny windows
allow fragments of sunlight.

An amber chandelier
warms the view.

The Golden Age

how beautiful it is
to see the natural aging of dear friends
whom you have not seen
for perhaps a span of 27 years

they still look like themselves
although time has continued
to hone their impression:
features now etched and drawn
but still it could be no-one but them

how sad it is
to witness the passing of time

once smooth faces now wrinkled
slightly on loosened skin
and the smile is an exaggeration
of the smile they smiled
when they were younger

you realize
your friends have reached their golden age
and, so have you.

you stare at them
in amazement, wonder
as they are several years younger
than you are.

The Golden Owl Heirloom

The old woman
handed her granddaughter the golden owl

    family heirloom
one and one-half inches high
round beautifully etched owl face

    exquisitely carved

    solid gold plump owl

strange instructions were offered to the girl

    inside this is a greater treasure
    if you are in dire straits
    only if you are destitute
    without hope
    and no other possibilities
    lie before you…

    melt the owl

    there are two perfect
    10 karat diamonds
        within,
        hidden.

The Heist

an ordinary Monday at the bank
in a small town in 1949
long before the internet
no online banking
customers cheerfully wait in line
they live in an old-fashioned world
pleasing and thanking

an ordinary lady in red shoes
stylish footwear for 1949
clutches a brown purse nervously
it contains a gun
shoves her way to the front of the line
she lives in a parallel world
sanity undone

an ordinary robbery ensues
rare for small town 1949
the teller reads the demand note
his face tight with fear
he hands over three thousand dollars
gun points at the frightened folk who
watch her disappear

To Awaken the Sleeping Dragon

to awaken the Dragon
kick the still sleeping dog.
Poke the bear with a golden log.
Jump off the bandwagon.

Topaz Gem

amber sunshine beams
sun topaz pendant
midsummer palate
tawny sandy dreams

Useless Treasure

A suitcase full of marked bills
Buried beneath the
town Hill's Bar
Weighted down with golden bars
rivaling the shine of stars
with no map
to show the way
rumoured treasure
is hearsay
December 1929
somewhere in
between the
Christmas time

Wigs and Gold Soles

curly wig cascades
in gold waves
tanned bare skin
above tight
yellow satin
black flat shoes
hide expensive
gold sprayed soles
green gold eyeshadow
black thick eyeliner
rose gold sun scratched skin
golden sparkling lipstick
drinks drambuie in sips
goblet carved from lapis lazuli

Golden Wolf Eyes
(haiku)

gold eyed black furred beast
disturbing in dark of night
are golden wolf eyes

Perfect Replicas

bouquet of gilded flowers
never will crumble
never will wilt

no artistic skill

live flowers
dipped in gold
perfect replicas

One Gold Tear

one solitary tear of solid gold
gleams upon the frozen island
of her face

travels to the deep ridges
of her right cheek

swims alone
to her lips resting place

she swallows the tear
and tries …
to speak

Think About Money with Affection

think about money with affection
hold a hundred- dollar bill
and send out love to the Money
it is lonely requires more affection,
needs company

any relatives
friends of
the $20 bill
$10 bill
$50 bill
go forward multiply
all the wonders that money can buy

show affection for the plastic
keeping money intact

the paper ones
are not coming back

Spell to Attract Gold

Imagine you are surrounded
by a universe of gold light
gold rays of light traverse
through the soles of your feet
up through your legs and down
through your outstretched arms
into your chest back
and shining into your face
and reaching your brain
tiny gold beans
swim through your bloodstream
healing offering happy thoughts
and exhilarated intelligence

Immerse yourself in a warm bath
imbued with frankincense, lemon juice, sandalwood
with flakes of genuine gold

later in the day bask in sheer sunshine
oiled in frankincense and olive oil
be careful not to fall asleep in the sun
you want to become golden not burned
spend one full hour in the sun
naked open vulnerable

be grateful for the gifts
of sun gold and prosperity
open your heart mind and spirit to wealth

over the next few months,
gold will be attracted to you

Buttercups and Goldenseal

goldenseal gold roots
wearing green plant suits

buttercups are kin
with yellow plant skin

The Fool and The Magician

The Fool and The Magician
live in a gold sky place
a common theme in the Tarot
King and Queen of Pentacles
rule under the same gold sky

Sun card boasts a sky of blue
familiar to the earth eye
of the querent
advised to stay grounded

5 card reading
what this meant

Crown Chakra

as the third eye opens
crown chakra embraces all goodness
gold energy, a master healer
gold fills the soul with happiness

the third eye sees
the once invisible
crown chakra touches the Divine
gold essence
gold redirects intentions
to attain balance

Heart of Gold

draws his heart of gold
sterling character
mind diamond clear
pure ruby vision

around
the royal neck
pearls of wisdom

topaz amber hair
alabaster skin
kohl coal eyelashes
turquoise painted stare

upon
the palace wall
likeness
hangs there

Greed

she sold her soul
to the highest bidder
taste of gold and diamond ash
lay bitter
acrid on her soul
strangled by greed
unsatisfied need
her diamonds and rubies
stone cold in the winter

Inside A Gold Vault

Inside a gold vault
bars of gold hoard
unimaginable value
unfathomable wealth

2 examples of
the worth of gold

194 billion £
Bank of England

6.22 billion $
Fort Knox

Moutain of Gold

mountain of gold
Ra sun god
fire born
falcon head wears
sun disc inside a cobra
ra say pronounce like ray
sun ray
mountain of gold

The Minotaur

        eyes were animal eyes
they carried a human expression
            he had wisdom of a kind
                  for he knew himself inside
                          accepted the fact that
                  he could never be anything
        other than a monster

                sadly
            the awareness sprang
from the human side of his nature
            the animal half pined
        for animal companionship

in the mind's eye of this creature resided
                beautiful pictures
            these images terrified his beast heart
                deep within his spirit
painful yearning

in dreams the minotaur
        clasped, embraced
            some other being

        he awoke with his seed spent
desire unquenched longing

the minotaur was idle indolent
        sole source of physical activity
            involved the hunt each night

        born with no conscience
            he suffered no remorse
        he knew no guilt
for taking tender lives

        devoured virgins
                male or female
terrified screams
        heightened his appetite
                spiced the warm flesh
        to his delight

the curse of the minotaur
        forced guardian of vast treasure
he was no dragon heart

        repelled by their hard nature
                he played with the jewels
        favouring ruby or garnet

        the creature never
learned to speak
        his own bellowing voice
                would rouse him from sleep

he developed the ability
        to scream and shriek
                an imitation of
        the nightly feed

within the slow thinking mind
        the minotaur perceived his soul
                he believed himself a god

                in his own singularly
        horrific sense
the minotaur actually was

www.ingramcontent.com/pod-product-compliance
Lightning Source LLC
Chambersburg PA
CBHW072107110526
44590CB00018B/3346